NO ANCHOVIES ON THE MOON

No Anchovies on the Moon

Three Score and Ten

Washington Pictures and Poems

by
Paul Boswell

Introduction by James H. Billington, The Librarian of Congress

SEVEN LOCKS PRESS
WASHINGTON, D.C.

Library of Congress Cataloging-in-Publication Data

Boswell, Paul, 1913 –
    No anchovies on the moon : three score and ten washington pictures and poems
/ by Paul Boswell.
        p.   cm.
    ISBN 0-929765-33-8
    I. Title
PS3552.08123N6   1994
811'.54—dc20   93-44800
                                                    CIP

Manufactured in the United States of America

Seven Locks Press
Washington, D.C.
1-800-354-5348

DEDICATION
To Libby, my wife,
Who thought it should be published;
And Tom, my son, and his wife, Wendy,
Who got it done;
And to Robert Barkin, designer,
Who knew the ropes;
And Norman Sherman
And Kathleen Florio, publishers,
Who took the chance.

TABLE OF CONTENTS

Titles of poems appear in *italics*; titles of pictures appear in regular type.

TABLE OF CONTENTS

TABLE OF CONTENTS

PREFACE

It would not be difficult to compile a list of buildings grander than the Library of Congress—for starters: the Vatican, Saint Sophia, the Taj Mahal. These I have not seen. But at the Library of Congress, "I dwelt in marble halls"* eight hours a day for half a century and tried, with dubious success, to capture some of its grandeur in the poems and pen-and-ink renderings of this book.

Paul Neyron Boswell

*"I dreamt that I dwelt in marble halls." Song. Alfred Bunn, *The Bohemian Girl.*

INTRODUCTION

The Library of Congress is an extraordinary place, almost a city unto itself, with an exciting life that varies each day depending on the flow of people and events. The special gatherings that take place each year at the Library number in the hundreds: poetry readings, musical events, serious talks and discussions for serious people, gatherings of academics and students in a wide variety of fields. The Library celebrates the life of the mind and ideas, of history and tradition, but it also deals with the facts and details of today, as well as the legislation of tomorrow.

One can sense its special qualities in the diligence of its resident scholars and the excitement of its visitors. The Library can be a wonderful intellectual experience. It is more than a repository of books and old newspapers, more than a home to photographs and manuscripts and recordings. It is certainly all of those things, but somehow the sum is far greater than the parts. From our earliest days as a nation, when Thomas Jefferson sold his own library to the Congress, the Library has been a living monument to ideas, to the magic of words, the glory of history, and the triumph of reason in man's vision for tomorrow. Yet even Jefferson could not have anticipated how it has grown and what it has become.

Today there are over a hundred million items in the Library, including almost 16 million books in our classified collections, over 4 million maps, 41 million manuscript pages, close to 2 million discs, tapes, and other recorded material. The Library conducts public tours for almost 50,000 people each year, and 8,000 professionals—librarians and others—come to learn here. For the nearly one million people who use it or visit it each year and for the more than 4,400 people who work in its various programs and perform its many functions, the Library is simply a place of unique excellence and vast resources.

One of the greatest resources of the Library is something that cannot be cataloged. It is the people who work in its great halls, among its stacks, in its offices, binding materials, restoring others, keeping order in an ever-expanding record of human thought, and who serve a million users each year and other libraries across the country and, indeed, the world. Employees of the Library have a special allegiance to it, a special affection that is sometimes difficult to describe, but always easy to sense in their devotion to the place and their work.

No one displayed that affection more than Paul Boswell during the 46 years he worked here, and no one I know has captured those qualities any better than he in his poems and drawings. Although he became an expert on government publications of Great Britain and the nations of the British Commonwealth, it is as laureate of books and ideas and artist of the Library's grand design and tiniest detail that he has made his creative work a wonderful reflection of our lives. There is whimsy in his words as well as wisdom; there is an expansive affection in the careful, controlled, and precise lines of his drawings. There is delight in this special place that inspires his work.

Many of Paul Boswell's drawings grace the walls and bulletin boards of the Library. Some of them perch on a wall or shelf as Christmas cards he sent over the years, especially cherished by his friends who received them. Ten of them hang in the Government Publications Reading Room, extending his warmth and presence beyond the years he served there. They have appeared in programs, calendars, and magazines.

I am pleased that he has now gathered his poems and drawings in a single book, providing all of us the opportunity to share with him his love for the Library and its surroundings. What began as a youthful job at the Library has grown and continued as an abiding passion. You can see it here. And I think you will like it as much as I do.

James H. Billington
The Librarian of Congress

Twenty-two National Capitol Columns

THIS SPLENDID SPECK
(A Small Hymn for One of the Smaller Planets)

There are no peacocks on Venus,
No oak trees or water lilies on Jupiter,
No squirrels or whales or figs on Mercury,
No anchovies on the moon;

And inside the rings of Saturn
There is no species that makes poems
and Intercontinental missiles.

Eight wasted planets,
Several dozen wasted moons.

In all the Sun's half-lighted entourage
One unbelievable blue and white exception,
This breeding, feeding, bleeding,
Cloud-peekaboo Earth,
Is not dead as a diamond.

This splendid speck,
This DNA experiment station,
Where life seems, somehow,
To have designed or assembled itself;
Where Chance and Choice
Play at survival and extinction;

Where molecules beget molecules,
And mistakes in the begetting
May be inconsequential,
Or lethal or lucky;
Where life everywhere eats life
And reproduction usually outpaces cannibalism;

This bloody paradise
Where, under the Northern lights,
Sitting choirs of white wolves
Howl across the firmament
Their chill *Te Deums.*
Where, in lower latitudes, matter more articulate
Gets a chance at consciousness
And invents *The Messiah,* or *The Marseillaise,*
The Ride of the Valkyries, or *The Rhapsody in Blue.*

This great blue pilgrim gyroscope,
Warmer than Mars, cooler than Venus,
Old turner of temperature nights and days,
This best of all reachable worlds,

This blessed speck.

ALBERT AND ABRAHAM

Near Lincoln's Doric Greek Memorial,
Hidden half in holly half in oak,
Bronze Einstein, in his marble exedra,
Sits barehead through the seasons, and observes
Beneath his feet a plastic universe
With nailhead stars; and seems, with all his brains
Chess-playing with imaginary trains.

Like the Smithsonian's triceratops,
Much swarmed upon, Einstein's accessible;
Children and dogs, adults and Presidents,[1]
Have stood in line to have their snapshots paired
With Albert and his tablet with one law
That's understood by few, but known by all,
e equals mc^2—destroyed mass
Times Speed of Light, times Speed of Light again
Yields sunshine, or makes Hiroshima fall.

1. Presidents. President Carter

Quotes on the Exedra:
Joy and amazement at the beauty and grandeur of this world
of which man can just form a faint notion.

As long as I have any choice in the matter I shall live only in
a country where civil liberty, tolerance and equality of all
citizens before the law prevail.

The Einstein and Lincoln Memorials

THE NATURE OF THINGS

Twenty centuries after Lucretius,
A century after Darwin,
And several decades after Watson and Crick,
President Saddam Hussein
Said angels sit on the shoulders of his men,
And devils on the shoulders of the UN coalition.

In the same week
President George Bush
Told a television audience,
"Stop what you're doing and say a prayer
For our soldiers in the ground war."

Neither Lucretius nor Darwin
Nor Watson nor Crick
Could have been elected President of either side
At the close of the twentieth century.

Triceratops and Holly

Smithsonian Institution

TV IS A ONE-WAY WINDOW

The people you see on TV aren't people,
They are images of people,
And images can't see or hear you.
They are deaf and blind.

No matter how well you feel you know them
They don't know you.
Images can't know anybody,
And the real people
Probably don't know you either.

An Anchor Woman,
And First Lady of this town
Through several presidencies,
Has been talking in my house for several
Thousand-and-One Nights,
But she might not understand
If I, a stranger to her,
Called her Scheherazade.

Today, for the third time in a week,
I saw the senior Senator
At the Prostate Cancer Clinic;
I recognized him instantly,
But he had never seen me on TV,
Or anywhere else,
So we didn't talk.

Brenda Putnam's "Puck," Folger Shakespeare Library

ARTUR (BRIAREUS)[1] RUBINSTEIN

He's ninety now—
A white lion.

A man not tall
But wide of shoulders
And tapered downward.

Eighty years
His arms have flogged the coffined harps—
Part wood, part wire, part elephant,
And part Pythagoras—
On all the continents
Except, perhaps, Antarctica,
While his legs have dwindled
From standing only seconds-per-hour
To acknowledge applause.

No page turner sits beside him
To turn his music for him.
His lenses no longer
Eat notations writ on paper.
All the hemi-demi-semi-quavers
Of all the Chopins and Beethovens,
Rachmaninoffs and Stravinskys,
Bachs and Liszts
Are branded on his cerebral cortex
And celebrated
By all five-hundred fingers
Of each hand.

                                        1976

---

1. Briareus. Titan with a hundred hands

Artur Rubinstein

REFLECTIONS ON REFLECTIONS

Wet Streets

Tail-light reflections on a rainy street
All point red fingers at my soaking feet.
Toward every place I walk, red lines converge to meet.

Potomac

The multicolored Georgetown harbor lights,
The greens, the reds, the yellows and the whites,
Aim where, at John F. K., I stand to view the sights.

Atlantic

Sea moonglades grow but wider far away—
Do not the law of railroad tracks obey,
But flaunt reverse perspective on glittering display.

Washington Monument

At Constitution Gardens you may view
Five-hundred-foot reflections follow you
If you walk round the pond for just a rod or two.

"The World Is My Idea"[1]

Of each bright-fan reflection, I can see
Only the line between each light and me
At one of many places where I may choose to be.

---

1. Schopenhauer, *The World as Will and Idea*

Potomac Twilight

BOOK CITY
(The Library of Congress Buildings
plus the Folger Shakespeare Library)

Domes Look Bigger Inside Than Out   I

Outlined against the sky all domes look small,
But viewed inside their soaring looks sublime
Compared with multitudes far down the Mall
Who look almost like ants at picnic time.
Domes borrow glory from the sky they mime.
They vary the percent of sphere they show—
The Paris Opera's has the lowest climb;
Saint Peter's shows just half a sphere, we know,
And "onions" more than half in multi-domed Moscow.

A Second-Best Dome   II

No onion domes or Gothic spires are here,
But domes like Wren's or Michelangelo's.
One's high—a whole gray northern hemisphere;
One's low—and just a pale green Arctic shows.
A church dome for the Capitol we chose—
Saint Paul's of London. Some have thought that odd.
The National Library's style echoes
The Paris Opera House; also the quad[1]
That Philip built in Spain as "Residence for God."

1.   Quad. The Escorial, Madrid

The Domes, from the Adams

Opera House, Paris

St. Paul's, London

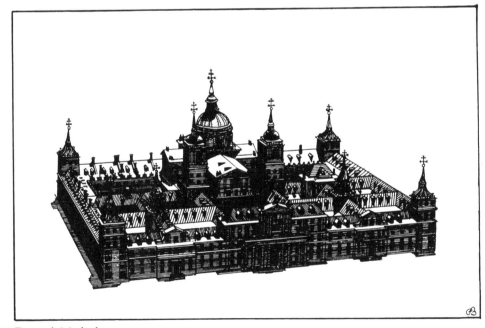

Escorial, Madrid

Skaters, Capitol Reflecting Pool

The Mother of a Family   III

      The Capitol was pregnant ninety years
      With bursting offices, John Marshall's Court,
      And copyrighted books up to its ears.
      First to be born, and of complexion swart,
      A granite bookery built like a fort
      Emerged to be a building on its own.
      Nine marble kin[2] of more Augustan port
      Have followed since, and to establish tone,
A private shrine to Shakespeare shares in this public zone.

The Tunnels   IV

      The Capitol's connected underground
      To three libraries and six office sites
      By bright-lit tunnels, like roots spreading round,
      Where tiny trains haul Members to their rites
      Mostly by days, occasionally by nights.
      The Rayburn-Longworth-Cannon root extends
      Through Madison's tall-as-Karnak shafted heights
      On Independence Avenue, then bends
Sharp north to Adams and to Jefferson, and ends.

2.   Kin. Three House Office Buildings (Rayburn, Longworth, Cannon)
      Three Senate Office Buildings (Russell, Dirksen, Hart)
      Two Library of Congress Buildings (Adams, Madison)
      One Supreme Court Building

THE THOMAS JEFFERSON BUILDING   V

Its proudly-second Greece-green[3] dome comports
Well with the Capitol's more towering looks.
This granite quad, at its four corners, sports
Four not-too-tall pavilions, like square rooks.
The triple doors of this Bastille of Books
Stand front and center, second-story height,
And spill their stairways, like cascading brooks,
First falling forward, then to left and right,
Past shaded picnic tables, with umbrellas green and white.

3.   Greece-green. Verdigris, vert de Grice, a green or bluish
deposit of copper carbonate, formed on copper, brass or
bronze surfaces

Neptune   VI

Green Neptune sits forever gazing west—
Rides backward as Earth rolls its eastward way;
As if He knows that what is past is best
And He has nothing left to see or say.
In the fountain round about Him, wet with spray,
And clutching fish-tailed horses, sea nymphs flaunt
Rubensian proportions, and delay
The more attentive tourists in their jaunt
To ogle or inveigh, if either is their wont.

The Odd Couple   VII

In Homer's *War and Peace* (that double book)
Our Pallas and Poseidon were the pair
Of adversary Gods who undertook
To liquidate Ulysses—or to spare;
But now, in upstart Washington, they share
An alien temple on a foreign knoll
That quite preempts an entire city square.
Its catacombs seem like a superbowl
Of books—and microfilms, grandchildren of the scroll.

Detail, Neptune Fountain, Library of Congress   (Neptune)

Detail, Neptune Fountain, Library of Congress

(North Nymph)

Detail, Neptune Fountain, Library of Congress

(South Nymph)

The Neptune-Minerva (Poseidon-Athena) Dome   VIII

Three scallop-shell coronas ring the dome—
Sea creatures, refugees from Neptune's pool.
The dome a while flashed forth a gold-leaf chrome,
But modest copper since has been the rule.
Minerva, as a patroness of school,
Is hinted by Her Torch of Learning on
The Lantern's pinnacle. These sometimes cruel
Rivals, Phidias himself had drawn
Under the western roof, above the Parthenon.

Torch and Courtyard

Detail, Neptune Fountain, Library of Congress

(Frog)

Bringing in the Tree, Library of Congress

Minerva   IX

High in the sanctum of a stately hall
Minerva stands, connecting earth and sun,
A fifteen-foot mosaic on the wall,
And underneath Her, Latin verses run:[4]
"Minerva, sans reluctance, has begun
This monument more durable than brass."
Eight pairs of small Minervas stride upon
The piers of entrance arches as you pass—
Sixteen Minervas primed for war or peace *en masse*.

4. Latin verses run. "Nil invita Minerva quae Monumentum
   aere perennius exegit."
   A quotation spliced together from passages in the
   Ars Poetica and the *Carmina* of Horace

Minerva

Southwest Exedra, Library of Congress

The Courtyards   X

Two sunken courts lie open to the clouds—
The larger spaced with maple trees of late.
A pair of auditoriums now crowds
The smaller court to quarters intimate
Where one may sit alone and contemplate,
With piping Pan, the goldfish in the pool,
View ivied walls, or, maybe, venerate
Stone-cut composers' names while seated cool
Upon a thoughtfully-provided concrete stool.

The Lesser Halls   XI

The rough, dark rock outside belies the sleek
White marble of those inner corridors
Whose gilded and mosaicked vaultings speak
With names and cogent sentences and scores
Of muraled myths the visitor explores.
Nine tympanums portray the Muses nine;
In other halls Greek Heroes play encores,
Endymion moons, Adonis bleeds supine,
And Arts and Sciences pose in a nubile line.

Whittall Pavilion Courtyard, Library of Congress

Pan of Rohallion   Frederick Macmonnies, Sculptor

Whittall Pavilion Courtyard in Shadow

Rock Garden in Winter, Library of Congress

The Great Hall   XII

Some fifty gleaming marble shafts arise
Above a marble chasm on whose floor
The Sun, in brass, with brass ecliptic, lies
Ringed with concentric scalloped discs galore
That imitate the skylights that out-soar
The ceiling, deeply beamed, with frets of gold.
Staircases, balustered with baby corps,
Sculpt crafts these youngsters ply till they grow old.
The galleries, high up, weave colors manifold.

The Great Hall, Library of Congress

The Rotunda XIII

Eight geysers of red marble hoist a dome
With eight-times-forty green and gold rosettes,
And arabesques in ivory honeycomb.
Moses and Newton man the parapets,
Along with seven other bronze duets.
"Religion," "Science," "Art,"—eight plaster dames—
Top off eight clustered-column minarets.
Within the red pendentives, on gray frames,
Glint Harvard's-choice quotations,[5] plus microscopic names.

The Rotunda (continued) XIV

The many-browned rotunda, brightly domed,
Has chocolate-colored marble at the base,
And caramel-laced-with-cobweb alcoves, tomed
With choice collections, in an easy place.
High in the gallery's encircling space
Loom sixteen bronze immortals—golden brown;
And, deep recessed, eight arching windows trace
Escutcheons of the States around the crown.
Topmost, twelve countries' proudest legacies look down.

5. Harvard's- choice quotations. The quotations were selected
    by Charles William Eliot, president of Harvard, 1869–1909.

The Main Reading Room, Library of Congress

Edward Gibbon, Gallery, Library of Congress   Charles H. Niehaus, Sculptor

The Collections   XV

Lo, pair by pair, in copyrighted queues,
Twin volumes file into this granite ark;
And magazines, by twelves and fifty-twos,
Reincarnation wait as tomes of mark.
Congressional pronouncements used to park
In ordered olive regiments to span
Eight galleries and their colonnade bulwark.
Here gather, to this amber Vatican,
The best reflections of the musing mind of man.

THE JOHN ADAMS BUILDING   XVI

As LC's graying palace number one
Had Neptune and Minerva for its theme
But now is called the Thomas Jefferson,
So building two, judged by its mural scheme,
Chose Jefferson and Chaucer as supreme,
But now is called John Adams, by caprice.
Macduff's pronouncement fits in this extreme
(Made at the scene of Duncan's late decease)
Quoth he, "Confusion now hath made its masterpiece."

The Owl Staircases   XVII

As the Capitol inspired our humbler dome
So the First Street stair flights to an upper floor
Inspired this entrance where nobody's home,
Up stairways to an elevated door
The Adams Building uses—Nevermore.
It would be a handsome eminence from which
A statue of John Adams could adore
Brave July-fourth parades before his niche—
For rites like these he had a most uncommon itch.

The Geoffrey Chaucer Room   XVIII

Atop its several-hundred-windowed box,
The Adams Building's gray North Reading Room
Has not one window, quite a paradox,
That makes it part cathedral and part tomb.
Stained-glass clerestories might the top illume
With brighter Chaucer pilgrims round the walls.
The extant murals we will not presume
To treat in nine short verses; one recalls
Four-hundred-thirty rhymes whose language still enthralls.

The Thomas Jefferson Room   XIX

The South Room is much like its northern clone,
Except the murals, half-again as long
As boxcars, differ. Both are walled with stone.
In the murals of the Jefferson a throng
Of matching stone-gray people march along
Against a deep-blue background. Chaucer cracks:
"Don't kick an awl, don't storm at every wrong";
But trusting Thomas Jefferson attacks:
"Men are not born," he says, "with saddles on their backs."

Owl Staircase, John Adams Building, Library of Congress

THE JAMES MADISON MEMORIAL BUILDING   XX

The Jefferson, the Adams and Big Mad
All have, in one respect, a common plan—
They all are oblong boxes and they add
A cube at every corner that they can.
The Madison, no thanks to the *Koran*,
Is cornered with white "Kaabas."[6] In between,
Five stories tall, slab columns space the span,
And slim windows, tall as flag-poles, intervene.
Each side's a white mouth organ, the biggest ever seen.

6.   Kaaba. The cubical stone building in the court of the
     Great Mosque at Mecca, in the direction to which Moslems
     turn in praying

Madison Annex, Library of Congress

The Flags and the Mirror   XXI

The Madison would hold eight Parthenons—
Quite sizable for annex number two!
Two flagpoles look like stainless steel, not bronze,
One flies the Stars and Stripes, and one a new
White-eagle flag on morning-glory blue,
With staggered V-shaped scroll caught in the beak.
The entrance wall of glass provides a view,
(A rear-view-mirror view), from base to peak,
Of the Jefferson's green dome—with wavering physique.

The Shattered Mirror   XXII

Or *did* reflect the dome a year or two
Until a vast bronze screen, over ninety books,
Some big as table tops, cut off the view,
Except where sky or black shows through the nooks.
Pray, as you enter, none of these unhooks!
Each tome is two-thirds open, out or in,
(A set of abstract waves is how it looks)
Their sculptures, more Matisse than Gobelin,
Perhaps are flowers or stars, or galaxies in spin.

A Cascade of Books

Frank Eliscu, Sculptor

The Madison Memorial Hall   XXIII

Enthroned before a somewhat shield-like block
Of curving dark green marble of some height,
Clad in knee-breeches, buckled-shoes and frock,
The seated Madison is dazzling white.
Finger-in-book, he speaks to be polite.
His figure is reflected in the floor,
And, in eight sleek square pillars, left and right,
Reflected, as you're walking, eight times more.
Teak walls show eight quotations you'd better not ignore.

James Madison Statue, Library of Congress   Walter K. Hancock, Sculptor

The Atrium   XXIV

Four walls reflect the Atrium to five.
The fountain and its plashings multiply
Their images and sounds and keep alive
A drowsy susuration. Coffered sky,
With boxed illumination, must supply
The greenery's fake sunshine—energize
The shrubs and ficus trees that occupy
The granite Mansard planters, oversize—
And bring our four reflections to our astonished eyes.

Cronbach Fountain, James Madison Memorial Building, Library of Congress

The Color Code   XXV

If anyone designed a baseball park
The way the Madison has been designed,
The bases, like the quadrants, for a lark,
By blue, green, gold and red would be defined.
(Two white-halled miles, with corners color-signed)
No such arrangement's needed out-of-doors
To fix your situation in your mind,
But with unwindowed sameness on nine floors
You need the colors to identify the "cores."

The View from the Cafeteria   XXVI

Although the lower floors are window-shy,
The penthouse compensates with walls of glass,
Flanked, here and there, by boardwalks in the sky.
The dining view's not easy to surpass;
The steeple of Saint Peter's granite mass
Sits at your elbow, almost in your lap,
And miles of house-and-tree tops, and morass
Spread past the silent Freeway like a map
To where the Rivers meet, and Dixie doffs its cap.

Audubon Alley   XXVII

The corridors are white and bleak and bare,
Except the hallway leading to the bright,
Diminished, second "Jemmy"[7] seated where
Dan Boorstin's[8] aerie opened on the right.
This hall's a scene of avian delight—
Horned owls and eagles, whip-poor-Wills and jays
By Audubon, in frames four feet in height.
For fun, his hamming rattlesnake stage-plays
With gaping jaws, a baby catbird's wide-mouthed ways.

7. "Jemmy." Dolley Madison's pet name for her husband.
    A preliminary statue of James Madison, from which the
    larger one in the Madison Memorial Hall was reproduced.

8. Dan Boorstin. Author, historian, teacher, administrator,
    and bird watcher, was the first Librarian of Congress to
    occupy quarters in the Madison Building.

THE FOLGER SHAKESPEARE LIBRARY   XXVIII

The Folger, just quite big enough to be
A trunk in which a Parthenon was shipped,
(A cameo beside the other three
Libraries that the Congress has equipped)
Is rich in Tudor tome and manuscript.
Great Hall and greater Playhouse may be seen
(The outdoor marble murals can't be skipped),
But the Reading Room's a semi-closed demesne,
Except on Shakespeare's birthday, when throngs stampede the scene.

folger shakespeare library

exhibits 10-4:00

Folger and Spruce

New Colonnade, Folger Shakespeare Library

Puck Among the Libraries

The Folger Alto Relievos   XXIX

Richard escorts his princes with deceit,
And Caesar's being murdered night and noon,
Titania and her Donkey are in heat,
And witches cook newt, lizard and baboon.
Lear rages in a fathom-square typhoon,
And Hamlet's sire is stalking near the Mall.
Here Falstaff is regaling his platoon,
There Romeo's departing from a call,
And Portia cites a law, a knifing to forestall.

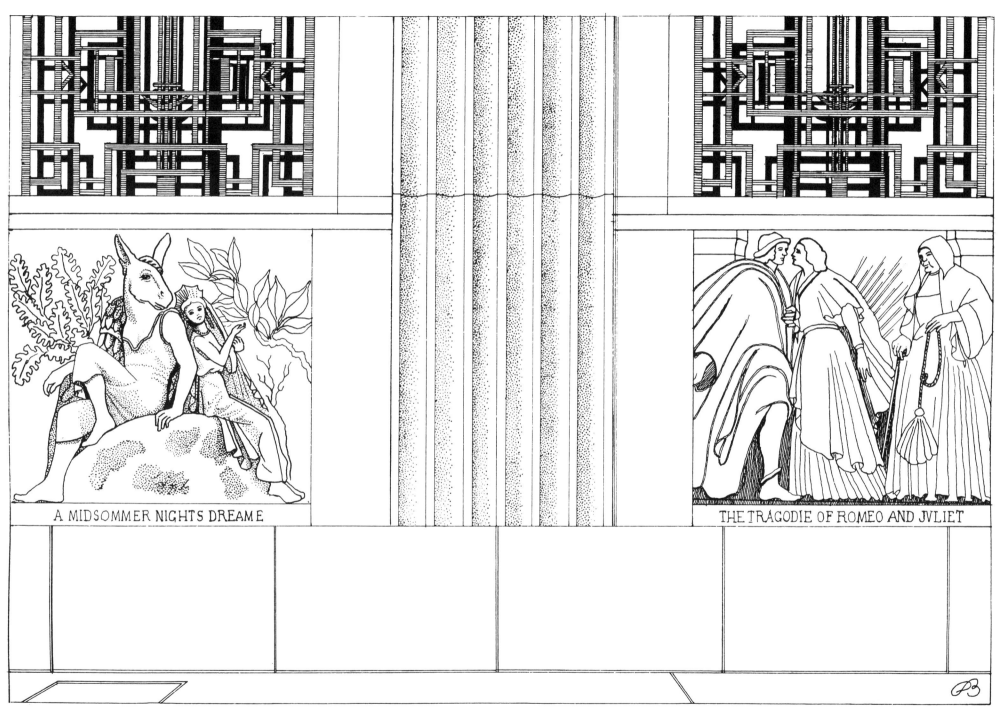

A MIDSOMMER NIGHTS DREAME

THE TRAGODIE OF ROMEO AND JVLIET

Two of Nine Relief Panels, Folger Shakespeare Library

BIBLIOPOLIS[9]   XXX

Four troves of books, that fill three city blocks,
All gathered in one cluster, are so rare
We feel like Ozymandias when he mocks:
"Look of these works, you mighty, and despair."
We have room for no more buildings anywhere;
We only can expand by growing small.
Newspapers have been shrunk to one inch square;
Ten million cards[10] into one breadbox[11] crawl.
We will shrink, like Milton's angels,[12] the Readers last of all.

9.   *Bibliopolis*. The writer's manufactured name for the three
     Library of Congress buildings plus the Folger Shakespeare
     Library—nothing official about the word, just means "book city."

10. Cards. Catalog cards.

11. Breadbox. Computer terminal.

12. Milton's angels. In *Paradise Lost* Satan shrinks the heights
     of his gigantic fallen angeles so he can crowd them all into
     "Pandemonium," his High Capitol in hell.

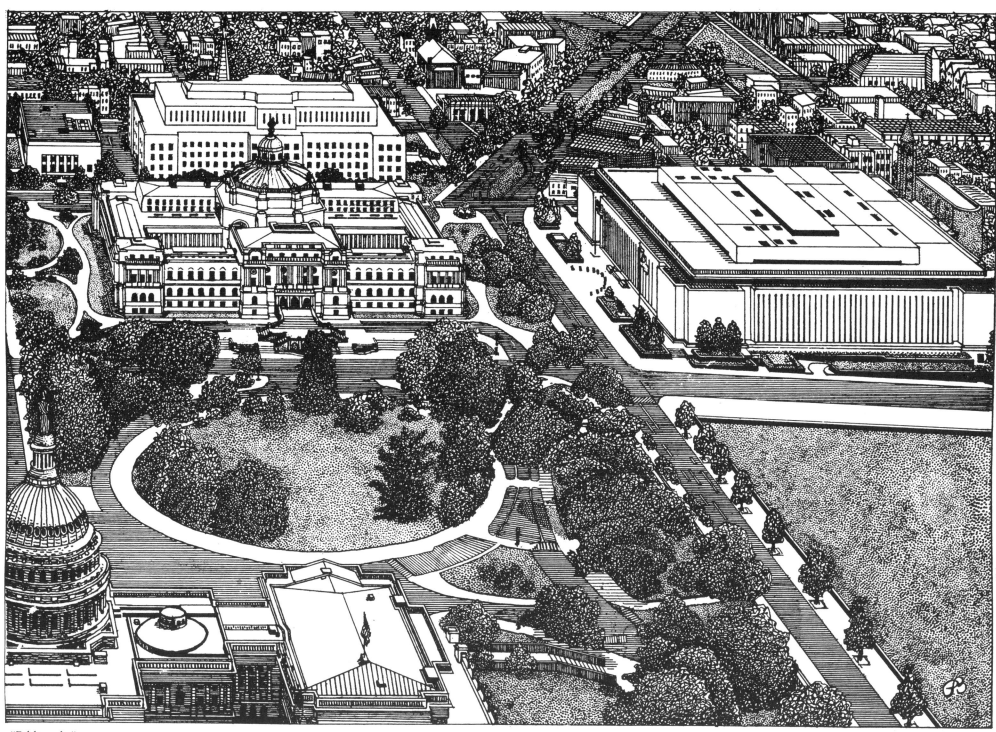

"Bibliopolis"

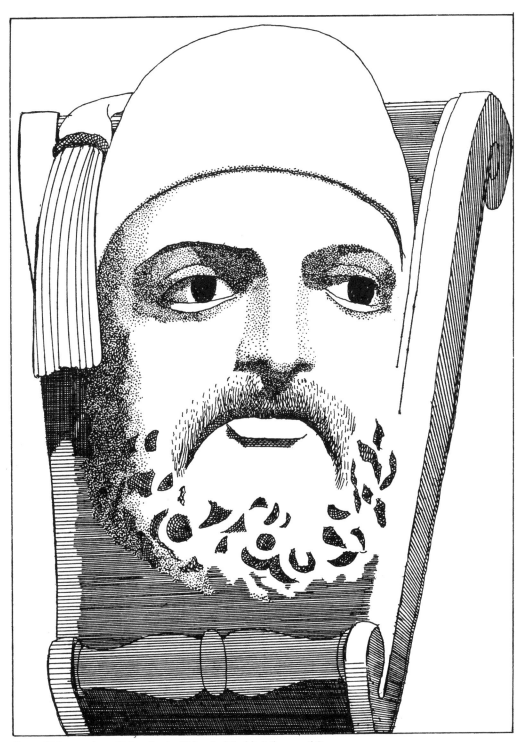

One of Thirty-three Ethnological Heads (Turk), Library of Congress

THE SMITHSONIAN CONNECTION

The Library of Congress,
Bequest of *fin de siecle* Congresses,
Palace of Culture
For the Senate and the American People.

Cartouches,
Much like those circling the names of Egyptian Gods,
Frame hundreds of famous names
And familiar quotations.

Trite Corinthian capitals
(Some granite, some gilded),
Trite owls and eagles,
Trite muses and trite ladies
Symbolizing Truth, Beauty and Vice,
And trite *fin de siecle* almost everythings
Are ubiquitous.

Only the thirty-three beheaded windows
(Keystoned with the granite heads
Of the Smithsonian's then
Thirty-three human races)
Were new to palace architecture.

Rayburn House Office Building and Botanical Garden Park

Hart Senate Office Building and Alva Belmont House (National Society, U.S. Daughters of 1812)

BIOLUMINESCENCE

Immediately in back of the hotel,
Where penthouse floodlights
Accent the whiteness of the surf,
The breakers are, of course, dazzling.

On the dark ends of the beach
Luminous waves are a rarity
We witnessed only once—
Breakers lighted from within
By a blue radiance.

Apparently it takes something of a bang
To trigger the light;
For when we stomped
Our bare feet
On the wet sand
There were puffs of glowing mist
Around our ankles.

GULL SHADOWS

In November
The only sun-bathers on the beach
Are fifty sea gulls
Standing in the sand
Between two old wood jetties
Covered now with granite boulders.

At noon
The sun at its sharpest
Pens each white-and-dove-gray bird
An inky-black companion;
And when the flock of sea gulls flies away
A flock of blackbirds flies beneath them
On the sand.

5 November 1979

BIRDIES

Smaller than the Capitol,
But larger, maybe, than the White House,
The Congressional Country Club
Is centered between the wings
Of the front and back nines.

At the August tournament
I sat a folding chair
In the shade of a wide belt of cedars,
And, as the famous threesomes belted by,
Heard erupting over the barbered hills,
(At irregular intervals of time
And at unpredictable intervals of azimuth)
A sound like gravel crashing down a chute,
As scattered assemblies
Of the forty-thousand watchers,
Exploding into applause,
Honored the latest birdie.

August 1976

Congressional Country Club

BREAKERS

Viewed from the beach, or from high balconies,
Most ocean waves are fluid satin folds
Easing quietly in from the skyline.

Breakers, not waves, are the exhibitionists—
Visually—audibly.

Breakers (exploding wave edges)
Burst *in medias res*;
Shrink bottom-to-top; stretch right and left,
Join hands, avalanche up the beach;
Leave beery deltoid wakes peaking backward,
Not peaking forward like boat wakes—
Tourniquets unrolling
To become frothy triangular neckerchiefs.

On calm nights the immigrant breakers
Are pulses of white sound and black silence.

When there are rains and high winds
And far-out white-caps,
There is a continuum of white roar.

THE TIDE ALSO RISES

Looked down upon from hotel balconies
At night, the six big light globes lined against
The dark wet boardwalk are six harvest moons,
Perfectly round, unblemished by gray "seas"
And not obscured by bottom-dragging clouds
Descended from cloud-level to be fogs.

But the smaller, gibbous, tireless moon upstairs
Drags the big Atlantic up the beach
And underneath the boardwalk's toy moons.

November 1981
7 April 1989
25 October 1990

BUCKEYE CHRISTMAS

In middle May
Vainglorious horse chestnuts
(Alias, Buckeye Trees),
Reupholstered in April leafage,
Chorus "Hallelu Jah" unseasonably—
Bedizen themselves
With thousands of white,
And one-foot tall
Lilliputian Christmas trees.

13 May 1978

Horse Chestnut, Stanton Square, Washington, D.C.

Playground and Funeral Home, Stanton Square, Washington, D.C.

JOG PATH

In this decade
Substantial populations of the young
Took to dope to blow their minds.
Others, in comparable numbers,
Took to jogging in city parks.

In the rectangular park,
Three stone-throws from the Capitol,
Graced by Ladybird Johnson's cherry trees,
And named for Lincoln's Secretary of War,
The beaten paths do not cut cross-lots,
They are not impressed by
The shortest distance between two points
But take the longest way around the Park.

Male and female,
Young and old,
Fat and lean,
Black and white,
Man and dog,
Day and night,
The joggers run rectangles around Stanton Park,
Beating deeper the peripheral dirt path
Six feet inside the cement curbs of the streets.

This spring the Park Department plowed up the jog path
And laid down a strip of green sod in its place.
The joggers, mindful of the exertions
Of the city's workmen,
Circumspectly avoided the new sod;
Some jogged just outside it,
Others just inside.

Now there are two parallel jog paths
Like wagon ruts.

14 July 1978

BUMBLESTARIA

The Boston ivy, a vertical sweet potato patch
That ripples the top two-thirds of our alley wall,
Came with the house when we bought it—
And may have been the reason why we bought it.

But the wistaria that screens-in the back porch,
Was transplanted as a six-inch cutting
From Delaware to the District of Columbia
Twenty years ago, and was my wife's idea.

Each May, between her birthday and mine,
The wistaria is a lavender cascade
From the second-floor back porch railing
To the ground;

And it makes a grandiose lilac-colored fountain
Draping the skeleton of the Mimosa tree
That died coated with ice
Several winters ago.

The family looks fondly
Forward and backward
To this flamboyant
Fortnight every year.

But the burghers who are really turned on
Are the multitudes of
Big black-bellied bumblebees
In ochre velvet vests,

Who assemble from God knows where
In May-Day mobilization
For hymenopterous rituals
In black and gold—and lavender.

LAVENDER NIGHTMARE

Three winters ago the Mimosa was gloved in ice and died.

Now it is gloved, more loosely, in Wistaria—
Purple cascaded in spring,
In summer a green octopus
Twisting the spokes out of the porch railing upstairs.

Yards of Wistaria feelers
At the ends of the amputated Mimosa boughs
Search for something to latch on to.
Sometimes they seem to grow a foot a day.

A yard above the highest feelers
A canopy of twenty-eight telephone wires
Radiates, like spokes of a horizontal wheel,
From the back alley's single pole.

If the wind ever negotiates a merger
Between the telephone wire system
And the Wistaria vine system,
There will be a lavender nightmare.

PARTICULAR HELL

Beware, beware of what you want too much,
The Purgatory poet gravely said;
In Hell you'll get it—have it in your clutch—
And learn that what you thought was gold was lead.
Paolo and Francesca died for lust
But rue Hell's blast where passion never flags;
And weary Prodigals and Misers thrust
Against each other, pushing moneybags.

Two years ago I died and went to Hell,
A bookworm's Hell, with polished marble halls,
Where endless miles of shelves in parallel
Hold many million volumes ranged in stalls;
And every day I pull them from their rack,
And every night again I put them back.

April 1939

Minerva Diffusing the Products of Typographical Art, Library of Congress

CALVERT STREET BRIDGE

Calvert Street and Taft Memorial Bridges
Form fragments of a high-riding horizontal V
Above the valley of Rock Creek—
That long, forested wrinkle that civilization missed
When it shaved the beech and sycamore
Off the District of Columbia.

We commit most of our suicides, here in the District,
From one or the other of these two bridges—
A suicide almost every other Thursday.
Perhaps it is as tempting a site for suicides
As may be found in any world capital.
Especially in the fall
When the beeches are bronze,
And the sycamores are gold,
And the fine branches of the beeches
Are like gray-white nerves.

White pigeons fly in the sunshine
Above the tree tops and below the level of
The Calvert Street Bridge.

November 1938

ENVOY

It's been forty-seven years
Since I last wrote about the bridges,
And Lord Calvert's bridge
Has been renamed for Duke Ellington,
But the suicides have continued.
In the last seven years
There have been thirty-five of them.
At that rate there may have been
Two-hundred and thirty-five suicides from the bridges
Since Duke Ellington was finished in 1935.

This is the place the world ends
In death by gravitation.

August 1985

Calvert Street Bridge

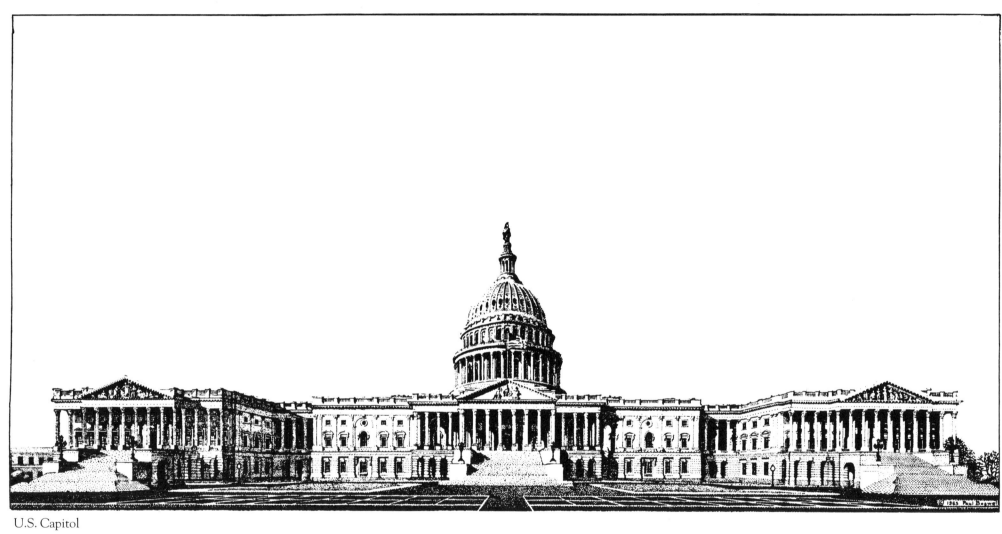

U.S. Capitol

"Democracy's Front Porch," George Bush

CATBIRD DOWN THE CHIMNEY

An April acrophilic mockingbird
Stops in the nation's capital a week
And from high chimney tops and aerials
Broadcasts his twenty tunes and then applauds
Himself by leaping straight up in the air.
He then reruns his songs and jumps again.

This morning in the basement as I passed
My turned-off, cold, gas furnace,
A chimney-top bel canto voice bore down
Through fifty feet of flue onto the floor.

I'd like to tell this singer, "Watch your jump,
Or you might end up like the dried-out puff
Of not-too-happy feathers that I found
When I cleaned out the burners just last fall."

A cat or dog trapped so would mew or bark.
What could that Floyd Collins of a bird
Trapped at the bottom of my chimney shaft
Have done but, maybe, sing?

24 April 1978

PARANOIA

Somebody touched me on my back. When I
Turned round I found nobody there.
This happened several times and got to seem
A little eerie.

The first I heard of the demented bird
Was when the *Post* of Washington, D.C.,
Reported that a mailman had refused
To make deliveries on my block. He said
A mockingbird attacks him!

For weeks the bird dive-bombed me from behind
Each time I left the house, or chased me to
My porch as I returned, and cussed me from
The rose of Sharon tree beside my house.

I think it was about this time that I
Decided maybe I should read again,
"To Kill a Mockingbird."

WORTH GOING TO SEE

"Is not the Giant's-causeway worth the seeing?"
"Worth seeing? yes; but not worth going to see,"
Said Samuel Johnson, somewhat disagreeing
With eager Bozzy, in their repartee.

Ambassador Tom Jefferson, in Paris,
Had a different kind of causeway on his mind,
Maria Cosway, his right-then Polaris,
To whom he raved of scenes he'd left behind.

The Niagara cascade, the Falling spring,
Potowmac passage thro Blue mountains and
His home above the thunder's bellowing,
Were things worth seeing, she should understand.

To see all these, he wrote with great emotion,
Is worth a voiage across the Atlantic ocean.

18 November 1990

Shelter, Old Olmsted Trolley Terminal, U.S. Capitol

John Flanagan Clock, Library of Congress

RHAPSODY IN BROWN

This Fort Knox of permuted alphabets;
This tank for all the grain of Gutenberg!

Green Neptune, on a rock, presides out front,
His Mare Nostrum just a puddle now.

And in a court, Pan blows on two long reeds
While balanced, like Fortuna, on a ball.

Minerva, a mosaic, shows a scroll,
A sort of antique college catalog,
That lists a thirty-course curriculum.

And the Reading Room's a marble hive for scholars.

Three-times-eleven keystoned windows boast
As many racial visages in stone,

And in round windows portrait busts of nine
Assorted worthies set a varied tone
With granite heads like Dante's and Ben Franklin's.

And the Reading Room's an humongous coffee pot.

The lamp globes clustered on the Plaza stairs
Are spiked like half-a-dozen Kaiser Bills.

The ceilings drop a thousand famous names
And trite quotations. Soffits vaunt leaf gold
And bright enamels.

Inside the Central Keep
The stateliest of amber study domes
Summonses a family of brown marbles:
Chocolate pedestals from Tennessee,
Cob-webbed yellow screens from old Siena,
Red columns from the southern Nile,
Thirteen hatboxes to each rusty pillar.
And a crown of sixteen Magi sculpt in bronze.

The book stacks are a paper universe,

And the Reading Room's a joy I can't outgrow.

EINE FESTE BURG

Granite!

Like Robert Browning's Gibraltar
This great heap—
(That Lucy Salamanca called "Fortress of Freedom"
And MacLeish called "Elsie")
This great heap is "grand and gray."

It rises in broad strata—
Rough hewn,
Vermiculated,
Smooth,
Entablatured,
And, finally, balustraded.

Its reinforced corners
Project wider
And rise higher
Than the basic Quadrangle.

It's much smaller than the Escorial
Or Saint Peter's,
Still,
As Martin Luther didn't exactly say,
"A mighty Fortress is our Quad."

March 1974

Amur Cork Tree, Library of Congress

ENCORE FOR JOHN THE BAPTIST

The royal family on the crimson stage
(Herod, Herodias and Salome)

All seemed, with towered tiaras, eight feet tall;
Their collars double-cubit wide; their capes
Swept round about the floor in ten-foot swirls.

Jokanaan the Baptist (in English, John)
With only scant projections, save his voice,
Impressed the King, but riled the royal women.

All this—Baptizer: fearless, resolute;
Teetering Herod; grim Herodias;
And Salome's gorgeous-grisly sacrilege
(Cavorting with the "Kopf") one could expect
From browsing Beardsley's drawings.

The Potomac presentation added its
Unique encore:
        Leave the crimson Opera House
With its electric-snowflake chandeliers;
Descend the crimson carpet of the stairs,
And, in the grand confluence-hall confront,
High pedestaled, in Banquo-textured bronze,
And Olmec size, the disembodied "Kopf"
Of John F. Kennedy.

1975

The John F. Kennedy Bronze Bust

Robert Berks, Sculptor

52 EAGLES

Fifty and two more eagles, big as life,
Stand elbow to elbow, beaks at "Dress right, dress,"
Above the arches, underneath the dome,
Supporting in their mouths festooning chains
Of plaster laurel leaves.

Fifty and two more eagles, big as life,
And the Library of Congress is so full of *objets d'art*
That you can work in it for fifty years,
And two years more, and never notice them.

16 December 1979
12 January 1985
20 October 1988

SUNBURN AT R. F. K.

My upper lip
Where my nose cast a shadow, stayed white—
As did the north side of my face
And the top of my neck
Where my chin served as a parasol.

But my collar bone,
South cheek below the shade of my hat
And the right half of my chin
Were red as cooked lobster.

On the beach you turn and cook yourself evenly,
But in the bleachers you are locked into one position,
Like a truck driver who sunburns one elbow.

The piebald red and white record
Of this afternoon in the sun
Will still be inscribed on my face a week from now—
By which time I will have forgotten
That the score was
Oilers twenty-nine,
Redskins twenty-seven.

1 September 1979

THE FOG AT THE END OF THE PORTE COCHÈRE

As you look south through the Jefferson Porte Cochère,
Bright day or dark, a white fog fills the air.
But halfway through the underpass you reach
A point the fog's top and west edges each
Turn to blue sky. The fog has now become
The fog-white marble of the Madison.

Porte Cochère and Fog, Library of Congress

Porte Cochère and Madison, Library of Congress

Porte Cochère at Night, Library of Congress

THE FOLGER

Petite paramour
Of the Supreme Court Building
And of the three Libraries of Congress.

Oak-lined and marble-coated shrine
Of Petroleum and Poetry.

There are no overt allusions
To the nine Muses
In this temple for Will Shakespeare,
But, for some reason,
There are nine
Tall, aluminum-grilled windows
Above nine
Fathom-square *bas reliefs* of some of the plays.

And, so far as I have noticed,
There is no portrayal anywhere
Of Shakespeare crowned with bays;
But there are four Bull Bay trees
(Magnolia grandiflora)
At one end of the edifice
And two more at the other end—
Enough bay leaves to crown
Not only Shakespeare,
But all the poets and poetasters
Who read their things
During Thursday lunch hours
In the Folger's Elizabethan Theater.

26 June 1976

FOLGER SHADOWS

From my desk I look at the Shakespeare Library—
Look at the back of it.

The front and the interior
Are as beautified as Ophelia—
Marble murals outside
Carved oak within.

But the back is functional;
Elevator shafts,
Bay windows
And terminal pavilions
Protrude almost at random,
All casting synchronized shadows
On the wall.

These Serendipitous sundials
Ease their shadows, slow as cats,
Counterclockwise across the building,
Pointing their fingers all day
At the slow Sun.

14 July 1979

ENVOY

And now the architects
Have filled-in the hollow tooth
With a second Reading Room,
And filled out the back
With a symmetrical glass and marble wall
Plus flat and fluted columns;

But the old Sun peers in the new windows,
And the metal mullions cast secret shadows
In a hanging inner wall.

20 May 1982

GOD'S BALL GAMES

A billion billion ball parks
    far-islanded in night;
In each a billion H-bomb balls
    ride round in armies bright.

And, near the nearest bomb we know,
    ten smaller balls of rock
In complex spirals ("world lines")
    perpetually flock.

for Tommy
March 1958

GULLS

Except at sunset, when they are lighted from below,
Sea gulls are rather unwhite by day—
Ratty brown, mousey gray—
And they stroll the beaches,
Unbeautiful as ducks on stilts;
Or stand in silent congregations
All facing one way
Listening to a sermon
By a Saint Francis who isn't there;
Or they sail the secret ski-slopes of the air.

But at night
They *are* white,
And sit on, or, like white bats,
Flitter-flutter over
Very black water
Just beyond the white breakers.

Relaxed,
Lackadaisical,
Perpetually on vacation,
Feasting the year around on sea food,
Sea gulls inhabit
The invisible Cordilleras of roar
That straddle the beaches
And wall-in the continents.

Navy-Marine Memorial Under Snow, Washington, D.C.

THE BLUE VENEER

Between black space and "God's green earth" the sky,
Some two leagues deep with bright blue atmosphere,
Is what we breathers breathe, or else we die.
Should it escape, we also disappear.
The desert moon has no such blue veneer,
While Venus suffocates from too much air.
Praise God or Chance, we'll have it just right here
Unless we foul it up beyond repair.

It's years since I have seen Cassiopeia's Chair,
Or any orbs save planets and the moon—
No Bootes, nor circumpolar Bear.
Smog even hides the Milky Way, star-strewn;
 Each living cell, green Kingdom or the red
 Must breathe blue air, to fire its daily bread.

4 November 1989

THE EXTINCTION OF THE BOOK

A writer in a recent Sunday *Post*
Reports the endless avalanche of books
Dumped on LC can never be controlled;
And half-way hopes the optic discs will make
Our friend, the printed book, become extinct.

Millennia ago the book itself
Made obsolete the chiseled bricks and scrolls.

Ecclesiastes may perhaps be wrong;
And "making many books" *may* have an end.

But, as of now, there's little evidence
The book's "Decline and Fall" has yet begun.

I certainly will not live long enough
To hold "Computered LC" in my lap.

So, for a while, I'll lay "Decline and Fall"
(With John the Baptist Piranesi's art)
Spread open on my book-board where it rests
Across my chair arms, and imagine what
Sonorous prose old Gibbon might concoct
To tell what he might think of optic discs.

1 October 1991

CUBAN CRISIS

With three billion passengers
In their back seats,
Mr. K. and Mr. K.
"Chicken" play.

MEMORIALS

Poor Shakespeare, by three centuries, had to miss
His Folger-Shakespeare marble edifice.

Dour Dante couldn't know Gustave Doré
Would make his *Hell* a pleasure to survey.

Pray, what would wry Abe Lincoln have intoned
About the temple where he's now enthroned?

Young Joshua-ben-Joseph, what would He
Make of a coruscating Christmas tree?

Jack never saw the Center "John F. K." is
And "Junkets"[1] never studied *Adonais*.

14 January 1985
4 January 1988

1.   Junkets. Leigh Hunt's nickname for John Keats

The Continents, America and Africa, Library of Congress

Philip Martiny, Sculptor

The Continents, Asia and Europe, Library of Congress

Philip Martiny, Sculptor

Pine and Lamp, North Side, Library of Congress

Puck in Winter, Folger Library

LUNATIC CHRYSANTHEMUMS

Like a funeral opened by playing
"Here Comes the Bride,"
The blooming time of chrysanthemums
Is untimely.

When the ivy has turned red,
And deposited separately
The red leaves and the red stems;
And the oaks have filled the streets
With brown paper;
And the grass is gone;
And the whole spring-summer-autumn
Syndrome of growings
Has irrevocably called it quits;
These lunatic chrysanthemums,
Bright as daffodils,
Having November all to themselves,
And speaking for the whole vegetable kingdom,
Poke out their sassy golden tongues
In a silent Bronx cheer
At winter.

December 1974

MADISON LIBRARY FOSSIL[1]

Three-score-and-ten million years ago
(A million human lifetimes)
This two-foot cypress stump, now stone,
Grew in a swamp—
Its top branches, perhaps, a little higher than
The present ground-level of Capitol Hill.

Breasts had just been invented.
(The age of mammals was beginning.)

The apes, with their books,
Were not yet even a gleam
In Evolution's eye.

1. "Cypress Log.
    The 18-inch polished slab of petrified wood is part of a
    log discovered in the summer of 1971 by workmen digging
    at sea level, 40 feet below the surface of the construction
    site of the James Madison Memorial Building. The wood
    appears to be a form of cypress called *cupressinoxylon*, a
    catch-all word for fossils of the type that have the cypress-like
    structures, and which cannot be identified further. The log
    probably fell into the Potomac River approximately 70 million
    years ago and was carried to a gravel bar where it lodged and
    became covered. Marks on the fossil show apparent worm holes
    and where branches used to be. During fossilization the wood
    cells of the log were replaced, molecule by molecule, by silica."

    Quote from the notation on the
    fossil exhibit in the Atrium of
    the Madison Building

MR. APRIL

Chaucer didn't look up "April"
In the *Encyclopaedia Britannica*;
If he had he might have written
"April with *her* showers sweet."

However,
The Muralist at the Library
Preferred it Chaucer's way.

His April, a Mister,
Floats above tree tops
And waters the earth
With an up-side-down amphora without handles—
A carrot a tawny-meter long
Whose dangling stems
Are rain.

12 May 1978

Aprille with His Shoures Soote, Ezra Winter, Library of Congress, North Reading Room, Adams Building

MONARCHS OF ASSATEAGUE

Assa-
and
Chinco-
    teague islands
Teem with oysters,
Wild ponies,
Black swans
And White herons.

They also teem with
Orange-and-black butterflies
That,
Though multitudinous in October,
Remain as invisible
As the partisans of Robin Hood—
Their camouflage the goldenrod
On the landward side of the beach dunes.

Clap your hands
and
Fifty Monarchs, black and tans,
Flutter up a foot or two
For an instant of
Startled visibility.

Rock Creek Minaret, Islamic Center, Washington, D.C.

MOTHS AT OCEAN CITY

Around the rooftop floodlights that create
A noontime brightness on the midnight beach
There were no moths last nighttime anywhere.
Tonight it seems that there may be a million.

When one of them alights upon a rail
Its wings are plain—unpatterned as a fawn—
But when the light engulfs them they're pure gold—
A million short, emancipated worms
Gone drunken with a suddenness of wings.

They dance a golden dance against the night,
Like crazy constellations.

EMPHYSEMA

It's two nights after New Year's, but indoors
It's warm as Spring, perhaps, or early Fall,
A temperature that most of me approves,
Yet I've been sitting on the frigid porch
Just so my lungs can sense the Winter air.

"First," Shelley said, "our pleasures die, and then
Our hopes, and then our fears." I don't suppose
If he'd been asked to list the pleasures, he'd
List merely breathing in the highest ten.

Yet, breathless, we forego the other nine.

I have to think it twice to realize
That all of us would rather give up sex
Than give up breathing for a half an hour.

As I round out my decade number eight,
I doubt I'll do much breathing in my ninth.
So, pardon while I step outside for air,
I have a rendez-vous with breath.

3 January 1991
8 May 1992

NOVEMBER BOARDWALK

The boardwalk is thirty feet wide,
Thirty blocks long,
And deserted.

In the November night
Before the first snow
I can walk, bundled up,
For three miles and not encounter
Three people walking or riding bicycles.

The stores and hotels
On the land side of the boardwalk
Are still filled with the trinkets of summer—
Popcorn machines, saltwater taffy,
Oil paintings, jewelry,
Mugs, mallets, T-shirts, bikinis—
But the owners have left Ghost City
To the solitude and the solicitude
Of the ocean, the gulls and the Boswells.

And on the ocean side of the boardwalk
The red moon lays its streak
On the black Atlantic.

D.C., 17 November 1979

ORCHESTRA PIT

At intermission
You may, if you like,
Drift to the front of the Opera House
And peer down into the orchestra pit.
Few musicians linger there;
But their violins—
Ten or fifteen of them—
With black neckties and amber bellies,
Lie on the chairs of their owners.
The violins themselves
Hardly ever have to go.

April 1978

James Madison, St. Peter, and Orion, Library of Congress

ORION

Orion was oversexed and really big;
He could wade across the Ocean
And not get the top of his head wet;
Or walk on water, like Jesus.
Now he's a constellation
And still doing both.

When Merope's father was slow
Consenting to their marriage
Orion raped her.

And when Orion took a fancy
To the Seven Sisters, the Pleiades,
Jupiter had to turn them
Into a flock of pigeons.

Chaste Diana took a shine to Orion,
As she had to Endymion,
But big brother, Apollo, didn't approve;
So he bet her she couldn't shoot
That black thing out there in the ocean.
She could. It was the top of Orion's head.
Wading again.

PIGEON SHADOWS UP THE WALL

The bell-less belfrey
Of Saint Mark's church steeple
Has arched windows open on four sides
To the weather and the pigeons.

As the pigeons come
Slanting down the sky
To land upon the sill,
Their shadows climb
Straight up along the wall
To join them as they perch.

31 May 1982

St. Mark's Church from African Section, Library of Congress

PILGRIM PORPOISES

Two weeks ago
I watched three miles of them
Hump south—
Taking two hours to pass—
Stitching the flat Atlantic.

Today, at sunrise,
For two whole hours again,
They sine-curved—
This time Northward.

What stories did they tell
    each other on the way?
And to what shrine Cetacean did
    they wend?

LET THERE BE NIGHT

This chestnut in thy memory be squirreled,
When judging Night for better or for worse:
"Day lights the world;
Night lights the universe."

Neptune Plaza (Library of Congress) and Capitol

Plaza and Parasols, Library of Congress

THE WISDOM OF THE BODY

I don't know how I heal a cut finger,
A punctured foot,
Or immobilize an army of viruses,
But finger, foot and lung
Know how it's done.

I have cells that in some way
Are better doctors than Sir William Osler;
And twisted zippers inside of cells
That may know more about the origin of species
Than Darwin or Stephen Gould.

Not every misery signals our demise;
Death's bound to come, but after many tries.

VENUS REVISITED

Dante

It's the Sun's blue mirror, before the Sun's in view;
Dawn's Lucifer, eve's Hesper, either one,
Or Helel, as they called it in Hebrew.

It leads the rising, trails the setting Sun;
Is brighter than the brightest star by far,
And brightest when its crescent's just begun.

Once Dante said of Venus, it's "the star
That courts the Sun, now from the nape, now from
The Brow," for him a trope that's singular.

It's planet two in our curriculum,
But Dante called it Heaven number three,
Where certain sainted sinners sometimes come—

Ex-troubadours and ladies of degree;
Rahab the Harlot there has sovereignty.

NASA

Last month four Venus probes, called Pioneers,
Reported that her red-hot surface rocks
Glowed upward seven miles through atmospheres

Of CO_2, whose winds a space probe clocks
At upwards of two hundred miles an hour,
And that its acid clouds, in poison flocks,

Were ten miles thick, and sulfur acid sour.
No ocean's there, all water's turned to steam,
And sunshine is reduced to candle power.

Air pressure also is a bit extreme;
It's ninety times as much as where we dwell;
Dense as at ocean-bottom it would seem.

It's Lucifer, it's Hesper, it's Helel,
Dante's Third Heaven, NASA's new-found Hell.

2 January 1979

131

PUMPKINS

Pumpkins have meridians of longitude
But not of latitude;
They have crooked north poles
But no south poles at all.

Colorwise
They look more like little moons
Than little earths,
And a single pumpkin vine
May have more moons than Jupiter.

The insides of pumpkins look like
The insides of cantaloupes,
But cutting them is like
Cutting wood or shoe leather.

Pumpkins live with corn
And die with turkeys.

Pumpkins are holiday vegetables
Foreordained to end up
Pies or jack-o-lanterns.
They celebrate with equal relish
The mischief of witches
Or the bounty of God.

20 November 1979

QUAKER OATS

Another Thursday at the Folger
And the poets
Are still running their words together
Like the oats
In cooked oatmeal.

It's a pleasant porridge,
And, it is to be hoped,
Somehow nourishing,
But it tells me just as much
As Quaker Oats.

11 May 1978

QUATRAIN FOR SPARROWS

The sparrows on the wires, poor dears,
Can't tap our phone calls with their ears;
But, as they sit and swing and tweet,
Grasp conversations with both feet.

27 May 1986

RED IVY

Nothing anywhere
Is quite as gorgeous as
November Boston Ivy.

The hand-sized leaves
Are lipstick reds,
Sleek bronze
And waxy yellows.

What else makes such a glory
Out of dying?

20 November 1980

OFF-COLOR AUTUMN

Some years the ivy doesn't die right.
Something was wrong with the weather
In the fall of 1986.
The ivy didn't turn red and yellow,
And the leaves and stems didn't fall off
Either separately or together;
The leaves simply darkened,
Curled themselves into vertical rolls
And hung straight down
Against the red brick wall
Like bats sleeping in a cave.

20 November 1986

"Don Quixote," Gift of Spain, Kennedy Center

Aurelio Teno, Sculptor

Final Psalm Mural, Israeli Room, Kennedy Center

EDNA

I'd rather read *Millay* than read the *Psalms*,
Shakespeare's *Sonnets* couldn't touch her,
She'd be tri-sexual without qualms—
Love men and women much, but versing mucher.

HUMMINGBIRD SOULS

Hummingbirds don't go to heaven,
    as far as we can tell;
And vultures, since they have no souls,
    never go to hell.
Souls, so well known in Plato's Academy,
    can't be found in *Gray's Anatomy*.

THE PENNSYLVANIA AVENUE FACADE

At the north end of John Adams
The cars descend and ascend by ramps.

On the east and west fronts
Two sets of triple doors present in bronze
A dozen gods or demi-gods or men
Who first taught homo sapiens to write.

But the grand, unused, facade is on the South
Where matching marble staircases
Climb to second-story bronze doors—
Doors that have stayed locked since installation
Full fifty years ago.

No one is ever on these elegant stairs
Except brown-baggers on clement noons,
And four larger-than-eagle-sized white marble owls,
Minions of Minerva, who peer over their shoulders
At Pennsylvania Avenue.

I don't know what this great non-entrance cost—
Surely it would buy a lot more house
Than you and I could pay for.

This I can forgive.

Without the Adams Building's fake facade,
And the Madison's Cascade of Falling Books

LC would be
One granite palace and two marble barns.

Pennsylvania Avenue Facade, John Adams Building, Library of Congress

ROCKETS FOR JOHN ADAMS

Four light fixtures,
Octagonal cylinders more than a yard tall,
Fabricated of green bronze and frosted glass,
Are anchored to the marble wall
At the sides of the three-door entrance
To the John Adams Building.

Half a century of rains
Have dripped green tails of copper rust
Straight down the white marble beneath them.

What once looked like a conga-drum quartette
Now seems four green-tailed rockets
Blasting off.

8 June 1982
18 March 1985

West Entrance, John Adams Building, Library of Congress

Rayburn Building Rhytons

A SCRAP FOR RUFUS

Winston Churchill and I had one thing in common—
Both of us owned a violin-colored cocker spaniel
Named Rufus.
There was no imitation involved, either way!

We never knew how old our Rufus was;
He came to us full grown; was never big
On alcohol, tobacco or on sweets,
And exercised himself incessantly:
But after fifteen years he, none-the-less,
Grew stiff and old and blind and full of sores
And had to be disposed of anyway.

For many years our grown-up son still left
A scrap of some good morsel on his plate,
At home, or other cities coast to coast,
Left it from habit, and unconsciously—
For Rufus.

1977

A PUDDLE FOR POSEIDON

Green serpent,
Green frogs and turtles,
Green Negroes trumpeting green conch shells,
Green sea nymphs mane-handling
    green hippocampi;
All scaled
To an eight-cubit green Poseidon
    with a green beard
But no green trident.

Without His trident
Poseidon is practically incognito.

You could mistake Him
For almost any
Naked,
Twelve-foot-tall,
Bewhiskered
Green gentleman
You might happen to meet.

2 August 1978

Henry Moore's "Knife Edge Mirror Two Piece," National Gallery of Art

Senate Nocturne

SENATE PARK

Campus without a college,
Where a Company of oaks
Stands at Parade Rest.

It is inhabited by:

Good robins and bad starlings,
Their good and bad heads
Glide forward and backward,
Like the heads of cobras,
When they walk,

And by black-eyed squirrels
Who seldom walk at all,
But bound and bound—
    Helices
    Up the trees,
Parabolas along the ground.

SPRING FURLOUGH, 1945

Last night hitch-hiking south to Delaware
I met Spring sweeping northward through the States,
And sensed and loved along the blacked-out streets
Her sudden over-ambience of green.

Tomorrow I'll head back to Buffalo
And there await the pale green second coming
Of the Spring.

Gwenfritz and the Obelisk

151

U.S. Supreme Court

Bethlehem Chapel, National Cathedral

THESE DOORS HAVE STUDIED LATIN

The front doors of our soaring Reading Room,
Excepting for their frames, are not of bronze.

They haven't anything in common with
Ghiberti's "Gates of Paradise," nor with
Auguste Rodin's as famous "Gates of Hell."

These doors are merely tall, and merely oak,
With simple windows in the upper halves
That visitors can peer through at us all
And at our red rotunda rising tall.

The only thing the least bit sculpturesque
Is a wooden moulding carved with holly leaves.

But when you enter or you leave this Room,
These Portals silently remind you that
These doors have studied Latin, please take note,
We spell it, "PVSH" and "PVLL," but never gloat.

A CASCADE OF BOOKS

I know of nothing anywhere that looks
Like Frank Eliscu's bronze "Cascade Of Books,"

A reredos very secular indeed
For which a top library has a need.

The books look like the nine-day-falling shields
Of Milton's angels from God's battlefields.

Like stars, these books are best observed at night,
When all outside is dark, and inside bright.

The silhouetted books then stand out black
Like the horse's head in Orion's cul-de-sac.

27 November 1990

TUTANKHAMUN CAME TO WASHINGTON

In the fifty-fifth year
After the celebrated dig by Howard Carter
Tutankhamun
(Born Tutankhaton, also known as Nebkheperura)
Descended on the city of Washington
In a shower of gold and lapis lazuli.

During four long winter months
More people than live within this city's limits
Queued many freezing hours
To wedge, body against standing body,
Through a gallery two blocks long—
Bequeathed by the philanthropy of one
Who sold aluminum and purchased canvas.

Athwart the colonnade that fronts the Mellon Gallery
A rod-square silken banner, gold and blue,
Flapped in the coldest winter yet recorded here
Until it rent itself in two from top to bottom.
The flag fluttered the features of a boy
With golden face and braided blue-black beard—

Eyebrows and lashes, reinforced with black,
Extended backward half way to his ears
Like cut-off spectacles;
Horned, Moseslike, his forehead sprouted,
Like ill-matched question marks,
The golden heads of cobra and vulture:
And downward to his shoulders
A blue-and-gold-striped headdress
Swept like a lion's mane.

By age eighteen the boy was dead
And thirty centuries ago!
Why did eight-hundred thousand chilled Americans
Line up to view the relics from his tomb?
Child with a borrowed beard,
What empires had he grasped
Or wrecked or salvaged,
That now, millennia
And worlds and worlds away
His name should tinkle still a household word?

TUTANKHAMUN

Player of board games—Senet—Tjau
Hunter of ostriches,
Pawn of priests who ushered back the creature-gods
That Akhenaton, Pope of the Sun,
Decreed should be forgotten;
Was it for him our late-born thousands
Stood cold in January queues?

Don't be absurd!
Eight-hundred thousand chaining tourists never heard
About his kingdoms, or his gods, or ostriches.
Yea, even Akhenaton is forgotten.

They came to lamp the loot!
The Things of Beauty—

The golden daggers, serpents, falcons, bugs;
And Goddesses of gold in gossamer apparel;

The alabaster lions, lamps and chalices;

The soundable brazen trumpets;

The ebony and ivory checkerboards,
And ivory headrest for the royal carcass;

The pomegranate vase of rarest silver
And the silver moon itself
In a silver-golden boat of fine electrum—

His Things of Beauty still an undisputed joy
After three-hundred less-remembered decades.

The King is dead;
His Things sojourn
From capital to capital among us,
Golden ambassadors;
And the lines of his Theban poet echo yet:

    May your ka live,
    And may you spend a million years,
    You who love Thebes,
    Sitting with your face to the north wind,
    Your two eyes beholding happiness.

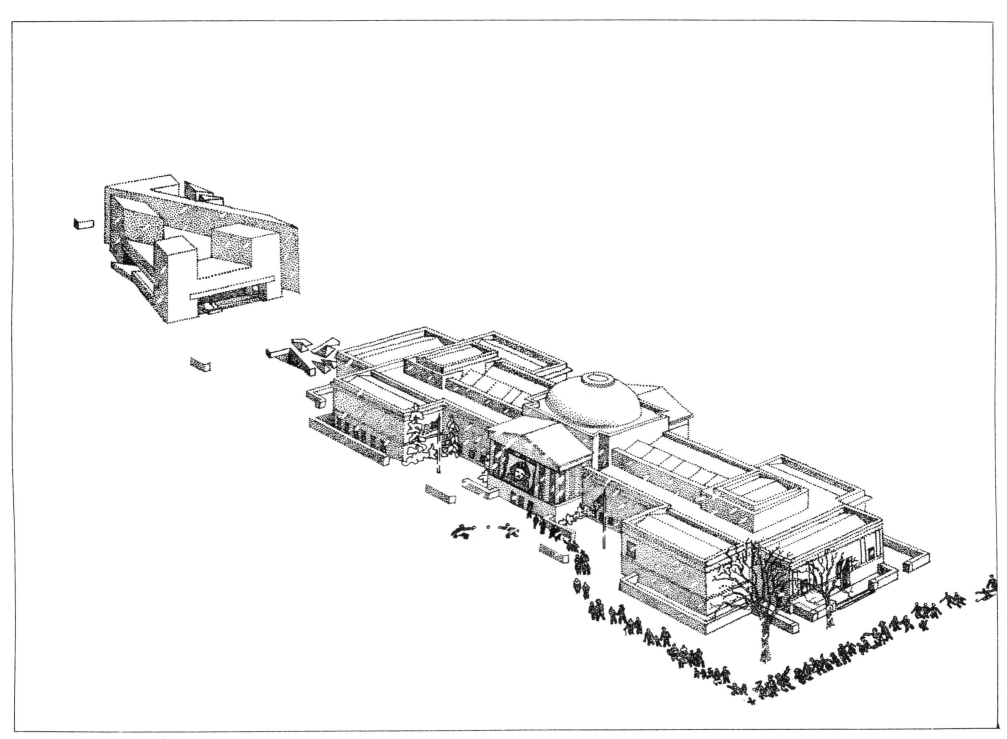

Tutankhamun Came to Washington

City shaped like the larger half
Of a broken Saltine cracker
The size of Xanadu.

City where statues of Neptune
And Abraham Lincoln
Sit forever staring toward each other
From opposite ends of the Mall.

City that has erected
A five-hundred-foot stone
Memorializing the Father of his Country.
At Night, flood-lighted from below,
The ghostly shadows of fifty flags
Faintly flicker the shaft,
While the pyramid on top, unlighted, disappears,
Leaving the lambent obelisk flat on top.

City where at night near Union Station
The velvety train whistles
Sound like the chords of a pipe organ.

City most alabaster of "thine alabaster cities,"
And most black.

City where Ladybird Johnson's cherry trees
Do more, one week a year,
To beautify the city parks
Than any dozen Presidents of the United States
The rest of the year.

City whose most-frequented monument
Is half-way under ground, a polished trench,
Where survivors see themselves
Reflected in black walls
Through a white curtain of the chiseled names
Of fifty-thousand dead.

My City, 'tis of thee,
Of thee, I sing.

WASTED RADIANCE

The moon has no known business
But to bounce an enchanting
Tincture of sunshine
Into the world's nights.

Eons before the waters spawned
The most ancient eyes
Moon light embellished
The blind earth
With wasted radiance.

The White House

FEBRUARY CAMELLIAS

Camellias may, or may not,
Be the most beautiful flowers;
But in the latitudes of the District of Columbia,
They seem to be the most gullible.
They don't have calendars,
They have only thermometers,
And are suckers for
A fortnight of February sunshine.

At least twenty of them—
Pink roses as big as saucers
With yellow shaving brushes
Protruding up from their middles—
Saluting a sunny Saint Valentine's Day;
Will be frozen brown as stewed apricots
And rotting on the ground
By Washington's birthday.

Others will freeze in the bud
As they did last year
When I picked off over a hundred
And counted them.

The leaves,
Glossy and green the year around,
Never freeze;
And the big flowers
Will try again next year.
Many won't make it; some will;
And several will float in white dishes
On the dining room table.
Seven Camellias will just about cover
A sixteen-inch meat platter.

14 February 1991
27 February 1991

WIDDERSHINS WORLD

This counter-clockwise earth
Is mighty special;
When it spins widdershins
The whole benighted universe
Spins deasil.

24 August 1976

YELLOW BULLDOZERS

Two yellow bulldozers
Back their rears into the ocean
And with slow, day-long repeated pushes,
Louder than the breakers,
Scoop the sloping beach to a flat sea level;
Heap wet sand in furrowed dikes,
Ephemeral man-high Himalayas,
Against the boardwalk,
Secure presumptuous hostelries
From an ocean
That may not always
Remember its place.

October 1976

PALISADE FENCE

One-hundred-fifty-seven unbent skis
Stand edge to edge. This graying fence surrounds:
    A living-dead Wis-mosa vine and tree
    That April loads with blue and bumblebees;
    A bush that arcs dark roses every June;
    A lilac, gray with mildew every fall;
    A glossy-leaved camellia; scarlet sage;
    Quick-coming crocus; and forsythia forsooth;
    Gray dusty miller; red geraniums;
    Red-feathered amaranthus five feet tall;
    And a headless *Pot of Basil* that I like
    To munch a pungent leaf of, day or dark,
    While rocking in the springy iron chair
    A moment in my postage-stamp back yard.

I can look east for six or seven feet,
And north for maybe twenty feet or more;
Then up one hundred trillion miles or so
At Vega[1] three and twenty years ago.

1. Vega. Twenty-three light years distant.

The Grate Society

Topiary Hare, Tortoise and Reader, Library of Congress

Gerald Garvey, Designer; Michael Burton, Fabricator

Christmas Candles, Library of Congress

Exedra Eagle, Library of Congress

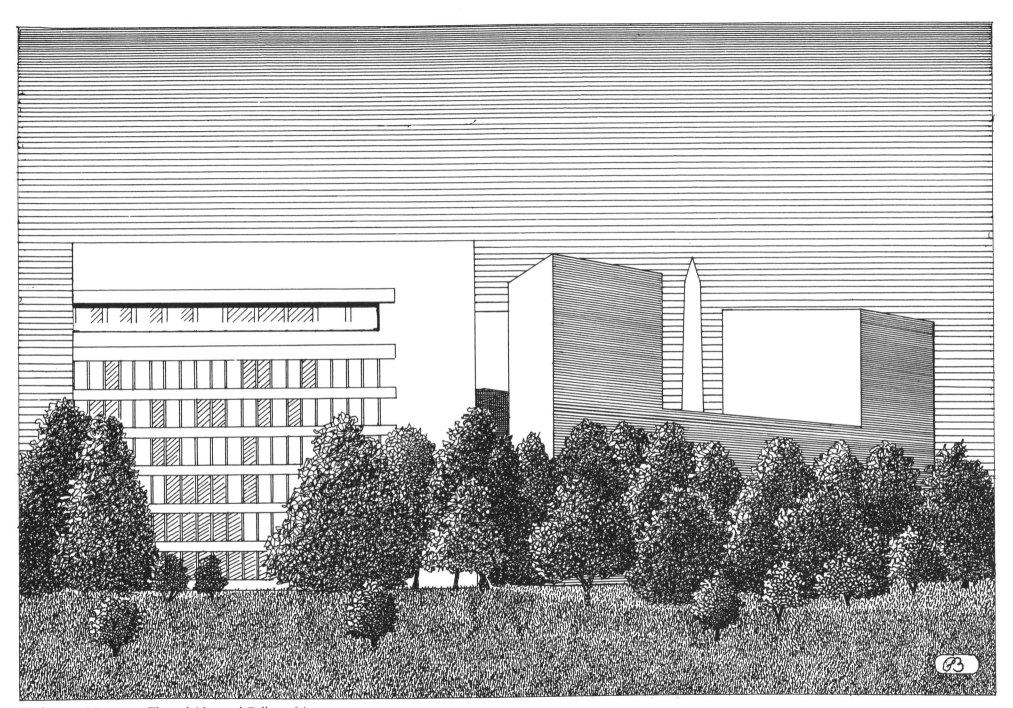

Washington Monument Through National Gallery of Art

BLIZZARDS

Blizzards of grasshoppers and blizzards of mosquitoes,
Blizzards of reindeer and wildebeests, and bison,
Blizzards of ducks, geese, starlings,
Blizzards of sardines, anchovies, squid,
Blizzards of spermatazoa in males of every species,
Blizzards of blizzards of species,
And in George Washington City
Blizzards of protesting or rejoicing mortals on the Mall.

THREE TENORS FOR AKHENATON

I had a dream
That from the Roman ruins
Of the Baths of Caracalla,
Fourteen centuries before the time of Christ,
Three twentieth-century tenors[1]
Sang "O Sole Mio" with all their operatic might
Toward Tell el Amarna in Upper Egypt
For Nefertiti and Akhenaton,
    Who disavowed all Gods but one
    And pledged allegiance to the Sun.

---

1.   Pavarotti, Domingo, and Carreras

AFTERWORD

By Thomas Boswell

No one got up earlier than my father. For decades, his alarm clock sounded at 3 a.m. By dawn his day was, in a sense, already finished. He put first things first. Like countless Washington civil servants in various government agencies, he gave his eight hours of professional service at the Library of Congress. But that was just earning a living. His essential life took place in those silent hours in the middle of the night. Then he wrote his poetry, drew pen-and-ink pictures, or simply read. Sometimes, he would experiment with oil painting or turn urban driftwood into furniture. But mostly, for more than 40 years, he drew and wrote. By daybreak he'd sit on the back porch of our row house, under a cloud of Pall Mall smoke, drinking his pitch-black coffee and watching the sun rise along the alley.

My father could never decide which he loved best—poetry, art, science, politics, literature, history, philosophy, or building his own furniture. So he loved them all. I've never met anyone more devoted to anything than my father was, and is, to the life of the mind. If he has a credo, it might be "I learn, therefore I am." For him, it seems to take no effort to lay down the *Scientific American* and pick up Gibbon, then listen to opera while drawing a picture. In fact, it may cost him effort to do anything else. My father educated himself with no particular object in mind. He was amazed that anyone would want to run the risk of dying without having explored everything that he was capable of understanding.

During 46 years at the Library of Congress, he spent every coffee break and lunch hour with a book open in front of him. He read *The History of the Decline and Fall of the Roman Empire*—underlining every page—in 15-minute chunks. He said he underlined so that, when he reread it, it wouldn't take so long. And years later, he did reread it—in 15-minute chunks in a room full of soda machines and chitchat. I've never seen anyone happier than my father reading anything.

My mother, who was as gregarious as my father was solitary, said she married Paul Boswell because he was "the only man I ever met who had an original thought." Sometimes you had to wait a while to hear those thoughts. My father spoke less than any man I ever met. I don't know if he ever actually went an entire day without speaking, but it would have been in character.

My father came from a generation that took the Great Depression, World War II, and McCarthyism straight in the teeth. He hitchhiked to get to the University of Iowa to study for his master's degree in English. He spent four-and-a-half years in the army, doing two tours in Europe and ending up a sergeant. It's hardly a surprise he ended up a serious, sober man. Maybe it's more unusual that he could still laugh.

Perhaps only a man this reticent and unaccustomed to easy glory would find it natural never to publish his poetry or read it to anybody but his family, except on rare occasions. He wrote because he enjoyed the labor—the countless rewritings and searches for the exact word. He would return to poems after years and completely rework them. As he sometimes said, nobody seemed to be writing the kind of poetry he liked, so he had to do it himself. Once he gave some of his work to Archibald MacLeish, then the Librarian of Congress, but said, "You don't have to make any comment. If I ever write a great poem, I'll know it." He meant the remark to be wry, since he was a modest man; but he was serious, too, because his aim was always high. He said it delighted him that so much of Keats's and Shakespeare's poetry was spectacularly inferior to their best work. That encouraged him.

He gave many drawings as Christmas cards to several hundred friends, some of whom decorated their homes with them. In an era in which many imagine 15 minutes of fame is their due, and where the thoroughly ordinary become celebrities through marketing, my father has always seemed out of step with his time and place. Nonetheless, I've always seen him as deeply American, but perhaps more in an 18th- than a 20th-century sense. He would have been at home with self-reliant rationalists with a taste for independence. He gave my mother a volume of Jefferson as a wedding gift.

Now, at 80, my father draws, writes, and reads almost every day. All it takes to stir him is to discover something he doesn't know. After nearly 50 years of work, he's decided that his book of poetry and drawings is finally finished. "It's as good as I can make it," he says.

AFTERNOTES

p. 1. National Capitol Columns. Columns replaced by new ones when the east front of the Capitol was extended 32 feet in the 1950s.

p. 3. No oak trees on Jupiter. The oracle of Jupiter at Dodona prophesied by the rustle of oak leaves.

p. 3. No figs on Mercury. Latin: *Ficus ad Mercurium*, first fig dedicated to Mercury, god of commerce—first fruit . . . first work.

p. 4. The *Washington Post* carried a picture of President Jimmy Carter with the Einstein statue.

p. 6. *The Nature of Things. De Rerum Natura*, a long nature poem by Lucretius (Titus Lucretius Carus, 96–55 B.C.) sought natural rather than supernatural explanations of things.

p. 9. Lord what fooles. Shakespeare, *Midsummer Night's Dream*.

p. 10. Pythagoras. He studied the mathematics of stringed musical instruments.

p. 12. Law of railroad tracks. The tracks narrow to a point on the horizon.

p. 13. Potomac Twilight. The buildings on the skyline are Georgetown University, the Soviet Embassy, and the National Episcopal Cathedral. No attempt at accuracy was made in the other buildings.

pp. 14–61. *Book City* (The three Library of Congress buildings plus the Folger Shakespeare Library). A 30-Spenserian-stanza poem, with 30 pen-and-ink pictures, is the longest poem in the book. Spenserian stanzas have the rhyming scheme ababbcbcc, and the final line has 12 syllables instead of 10.

p. 20. Homer's *War and Peace*. His *Iliad* and *Odyssey*.

p. 41. Used to park. Congressional documents have been moved to the Madison Building.

p. 42. Four-hundred-thirty rhymes. *Prologue* to the *Canterbury Tales*.

p. 47. A Cascade of Books. See also p. 155.

p. 51. The author is at the center of the drawing, snapping a picture.

p. 52. The Rivers meet. The Potomac and Anacostia rivers.

p. 59. The nine *bas reliefs* fit the nine-lined Spenserian stanza.

p. 67. Inky-black companion. Pigeon shadow.

p. 70. *In medias res*. In the middle of things.

p. 70. Deltoid wakes. Delta-shaped wakes.

p. 71. Tide Also Rises. *Ecclesiastes* and Hemingway, "The Sun Also Rises."

p. 76. *Bumblestaria*. Bumblebees and Wistaria.

p. 78. Purgatory poet. Dante.

p. 79. Minerva diffusing. Deck attendants at the Library of Congress, some of whom have postgraduate degrees, may find the *bas relief* condescending. It seemed appropriate to be paired with *Particular Hell*.

p. 84. Acrophilic mockingbird. Height-loving mockingbird.

p. 88. The boy on the right in the drawing accidentally came to resemble my son, Tom; so I added a "crew cut" of the kind he then wore.

p. 89. Mare Nostrum. Our Sea, the Mediterranean Sea.

p. 92. Kopf. *Head* in German, the language of the opera *Salome*.

p. 99. Petroleum and Poetry. Henry Clay Folger was an oil man.

p. 128. Neptune Plaza. This drawing was an exercise in using lines that were implied rather than explicit.

p. 129. Plaza and Parasols. This drawing was printed on the cachet envelopes provided by the Library of Congress Philatelic Club as envelopes on which to glue the first-day postage stamps depicting the Library of Congress.

p. 130. Twisted zippers. The DNA double helix.

p. 131. *Venus Revisited*. Venus as seen by Dante in the *Paradiso*, and by the Pioneer Space Probe. The piece is in terza rima, the chain-link-triplet rhyming scheme, aba, bcb, cdc, ded, etc., used by Dante in the *Commedia*.

p. 136. "Don Quixote." The sculptor chose to present Rosinante with his left front hoof missing. In the Battle of Lepanto, under the command of Don John of Austria, Cervantes himself was shot in the arm or hand and permanently lost the use of his left hand.

p. 151. Gwenfritz. Stabile named for the donor, Mrs. Gwendolyn Cafritz, at the National Museum of History and Technology. Sculptor, Alexander Calder.

p. 153. Bethlehem Chapel. Admiral Dewey is buried under the rectangle in the floor.

p. 155. *A Cascade of Books*. See also p. 47.

p. 159. Xanadu. Samuel Taylor Coleridge, "Kubla Khan."

"In Xanadu did Kubla Khan
A stately pleasure dome decree . . .
So *twice five miles* of fertile ground
By walls and towers were girdled round."

p. 163. *Widdershins*. Before there were dial-face clocks, "deasil" meant clockwise and "widdershins" meant counter-clockwise.

p. 165. Wis-mosa. A wistaria-covered mimosa tree.

p. 167. Topiary Hare, Tortoise, and Reader. Designed by Gerald Garvey, Chief of Library Support Services Office; constructed by Michael Burton, foreman of the Library of Congress grounds crew.

p. 172. Tenors. The three tenors actually did sing "O Sole Mio" with all their operatic might from the Batha of Caracalla. Probably none of them was thinking about Akhenaton.

SUBJECT INDEX

INDEX OF POEMS

INDEX OF PICTURES